The Love Card Book.

I have something to tell you.

It's VERY important.

The message is simple.

Are you ready for

this important message?

Ok, here it comes...

The message is:

You.

Are.

Loved.

That's it.

That's the whole message.

It's a short message.

But it's an important message.

It's a message that

can be easy to forget.

It's also a message...

That can be so easily shared!!!

DO IT!

Give this *Love Card Book*

to someone you know well, or...

Give this *Love Card Book*

To someone you do not know at all.

Because either way,

this important message,

Is so easy to share!

And always remember:

You are loved.

~~The end~~

to be continued ...

You may be the lucky first person to receive this copy of this book. Or you may be a lucky person that is receiving this book after receiving it from someone else.

Draw, create, imagine, uplift, inspire, and add your own creativity to the blank spaces in the book. Filling the pages with a piece of the next chapter that you are helping to write in the story called Life.

Or if you're more inspired to pass this book on just as it is, do that now! and grab a new copy when you're ready to share more love

The LoveCard Book

The first thoughts of creating this book came to me at a dark and depressing time. I realized what a difference it would make in that moment to be reminded that I, like all of us, am loved and deserve that love. And by turning towards that message within myself I realized I wasn't the only one that needed to get this message, and *The LoveCard Book* was born.

After all, not EVERYTHING that's highly contagious (like viruses) are bad for you - love, patience, kindness, and enthusiasm are ALL things that are HIGHLY contagious and everyone can spread!

Scan the PINK QR code on the back of this book to order more copies of this book and also learn about the GoFundMe Spread the Love campaign that will utilize donations to distribute copies of the book to hospitals, schools, and other locations where spreading smiles is needed.

Josh Yoshi Portuondo-Dember, author

52839853R00033